WITHDRAWN

I Made It Myself!

Paper Folding Fun

Didier Boursin

GARETH**STEVENS**

GS

PUBLISHING

A Member of the WRC Media Family of Companies

I want to thank my children, Nina and Angelo, who helped me, with a lot of enthusiasm, through every step of this book. Thanks also to Christophe for his valuable help. — D. B.

The author and publishers thank Fabrice for the photographs.

Please visit our web site at: www.garethstevens.com
For a free color catalog describing Gareth Stevens Publishing's
list of high-quality books and multimedia programs, call
1-800-542-2595 (USA) or 1-800-387-3178 (Canada).
Gareth Stevens Publishing's fax: (414) 332-3567.

Library of Congress Cataloging-in-Publication Data

Boursin, Didier.
    [Pliages magiques. English]
    Paper folding fun / Didier Boursin.
       p. cm. — (I made it myself!)
     ISBN 0-8368-5965-0 (lib. bdg.)
     1. Paper work—Juvenile literature. I. Title.
    II. Series.
    TT870.B657   2005
    736'.98—dc22   2005046498

This edition first published in 2006 by
Gareth Stevens Publishing
A Member of the WRC Media Family of Companies
330 West Olive Street, Suite 100
Milwaukee, Wisconsin 53212 USA

This U.S. edition copyright © 2006 by Gareth Stevens, Inc.
Original edition first published by Larousse-Bordas, Paris,
France, under the title *Tout en papier: Pliages Magiques*,
copyright © Dessain et Tolra / Larousse, Paris 2004.

Photography: Cactus Studio
Translation: Muriel Castille
English text: Dorothy L. Gibbs
Gareth Stevens series editor: Dorothy L. Gibbs
Gareth Stevens art direction and cover design: Tammy West
Gareth Stevens graphic design: Jenni Gaylord

Printed in the United States of America

1 2 3 4 5 6 7 8 9 09 08 07 06 05

CONTENTS

Folding Lessons

People have been folding paper into decorative figures for centuries. The Japanese word "origami" is a well-known name for the art of paper folding. On these two pages, you will find some basic information about paper folding. After studying this information, try some of the folding projects, carefully following the diagrams and explanations for each one. Before you know it, paper will change magically between your fingers.

PAPER

You should use 4- to 6-inch (10- to 15-centimeter) squares of paper for most of the projects in this book. The shape of the paper (either a square or a half-square) is specified at the beginning of each group of instructions. Some of the projects, such as Little Envelope (page 8) or Folded Frame (page 14), require larger squares with about 8-inch (20-cm) sides. Choose paper that is not too thick but is heavy enough to hold the folds, or creases, well.

FOLDING

Understanding the difference between "fold the paper" and "precrease the paper" is very important. In the first case, you keep the paper folded after you crease it. In the second case, you unfold the paper after creasing it. The diagrams in this book show the direction of folds with arrows and identify points that you will join, two by two, with dots. The symbols and diagrams on the next page will get you started.

(See page 24 for diagrams of special folds.)

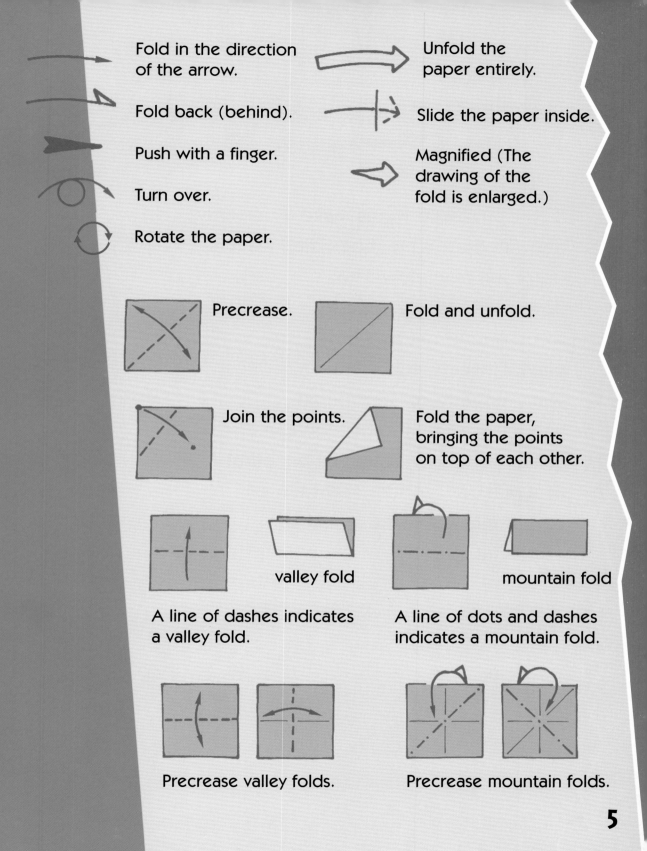

Fold in the direction of the arrow.

Unfold the paper entirely.

Fold back (behind).

Slide the paper inside.

Push with a finger.

Magnified (The drawing of the fold is enlarged.)

Turn over.

Rotate the paper.

Precrease.

Fold and unfold.

Join the points.

Fold the paper, bringing the points on top of each other.

valley fold

mountain fold

A line of dashes indicates a valley fold.

A line of dots and dashes indicates a mountain fold.

Precrease valley folds.

Precrease mountain folds.

5

Playful Butterfly

Brightly colored wings make a butterfly one of nature's most beautiful insects. Fluttering from flower to flower, a butterfly appears to be one of nature's most playful insects, too. With some brightly colored paper and a few simple folds, you can make a butterfly almost as beautiful as a real one. And a slight tap of your finger will make it almost as playful.

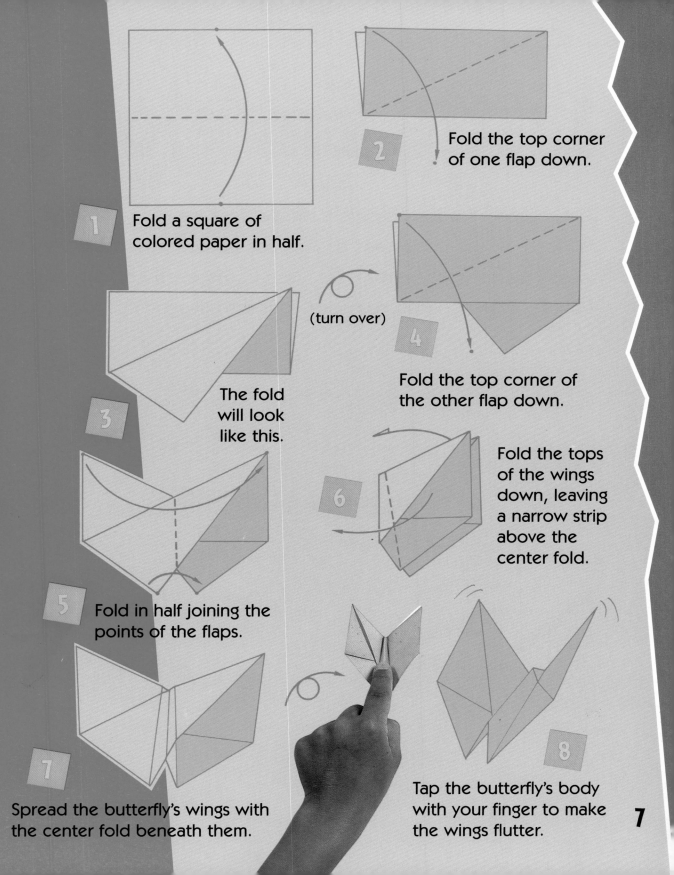

1 Fold a square of colored paper in half.

2 Fold the top corner of one flap down.

(turn over)

3 The fold will look like this.

4 Fold the top corner of the other flap down.

5 Fold in half joining the points of the flaps.

6 Fold the tops of the wings down, leaving a narrow strip above the center fold.

7 Spread the butterfly's wings with the center fold beneath them.

8 Tap the butterfly's body with your finger to make the wings flutter.

7

Little Envelope

This easy-to-fold envelope is the perfect way to give short notes or special drawings to Mom or Dad or to send secret messages to your best friend. You could even add a few fragrant flower petals to make your envelope smell good.

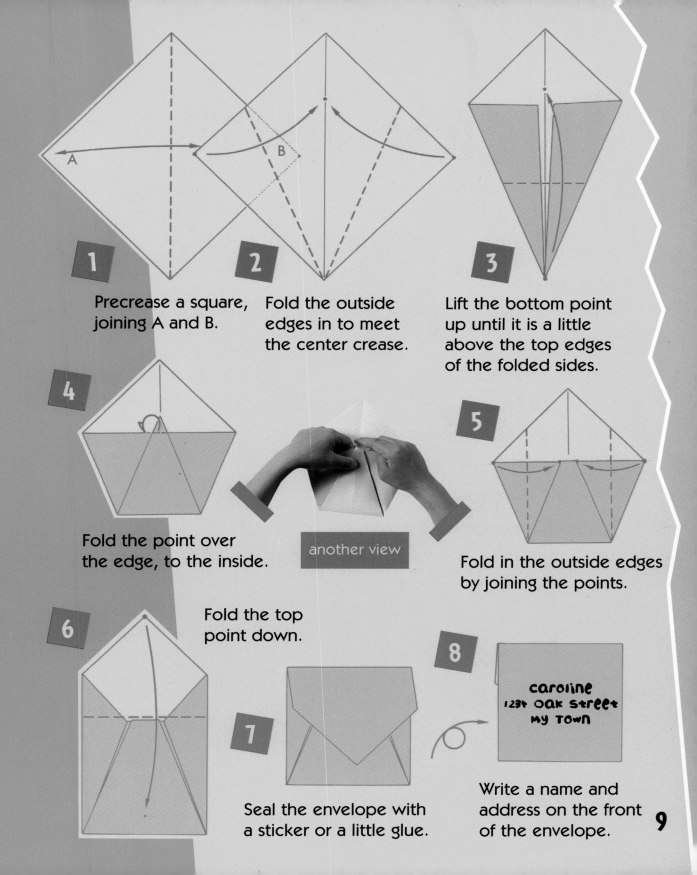

1 Precrease a square, joining A and B.

2 Fold the outside edges in to meet the center crease.

3 Lift the bottom point up until it is a little above the top edges of the folded sides.

4 Fold the point over the edge, to the inside.

another view

5 Fold in the outside edges by joining the points.

Fold the top point down.

6

7 Seal the envelope with a sticker or a little glue.

8 Write a name and address on the front of the envelope.

caroline
1234 oak street
my town

9

Tricky Turtle

In the wild, turtles sometimes live one hundred years! If you use sturdy paper, this folded turtle will have a long life, too. Making this turtle might be a little tricky, so be sure to follow all of the instructions carefully.

1

Cut a paper square in half and fold the top corners down.

2

Unfold the paper.

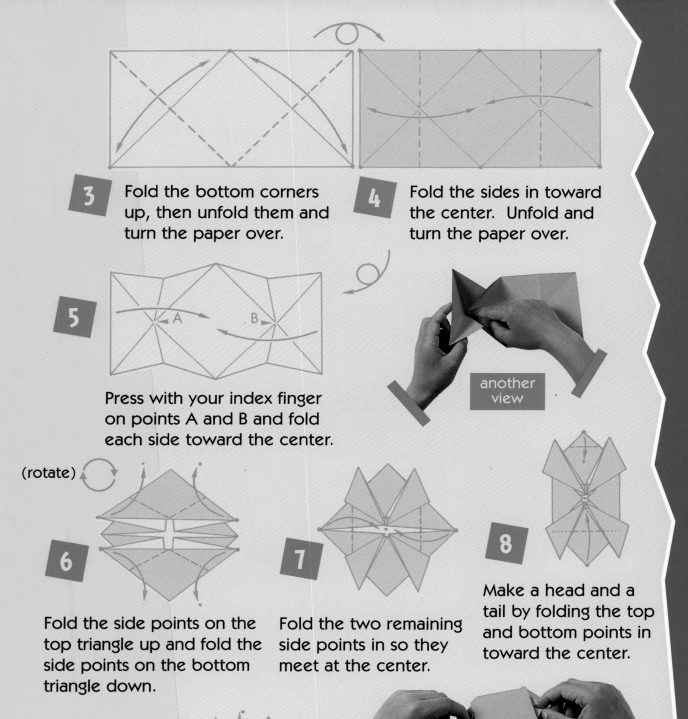

3 Fold the bottom corners up, then unfold them and turn the paper over.

4 Fold the sides in toward the center. Unfold and turn the paper over.

5 Press with your index finger on points A and B and fold each side toward the center.

another view

(rotate)

6 Fold the side points on the top triangle up and fold the side points on the bottom triangle down.

7 Fold the two remaining side points in so they meet at the center.

8 Make a head and a tail by folding the top and bottom points in toward the center.

9 Fold these same points in half, outward, then turn the turtle over.

10 Slightly open the head by putting your fingers into the fold and pinch the center of the tail.

11

Frog Jumpers

Some people say that a jumping green frog is a sign of rain. These folded frogs are sure to jump, so, if you don't want rain, don't make them green!

2

Fold the two top points back.

1

Find the center of a paper square by joining points A and B, then points C and D. Pinch the center point and unfold the paper. Fold points A, B, C, and D in to the center.

B

C

D

A

3

Fold half of the top triangle (1) up, then fold both sides (2) in so they meet at the center.

4

Fold the bottom up to the center point.

5

Fold down the two top corners of the bottom fold.

6

Holding points A and B between your thumbs and your index fingers, pull the inside folds outward.

7

Fold the points of the bottom fold down.

8

The folds will now look like this. Turn the paper over.

9

For each eye, fold square 1 in half and unfold, as shown on this diagram. Then, open the fold, as shown in square 2, folding it in half.

10

Press your index finger where the circle is on this diagram to make the frog jump.

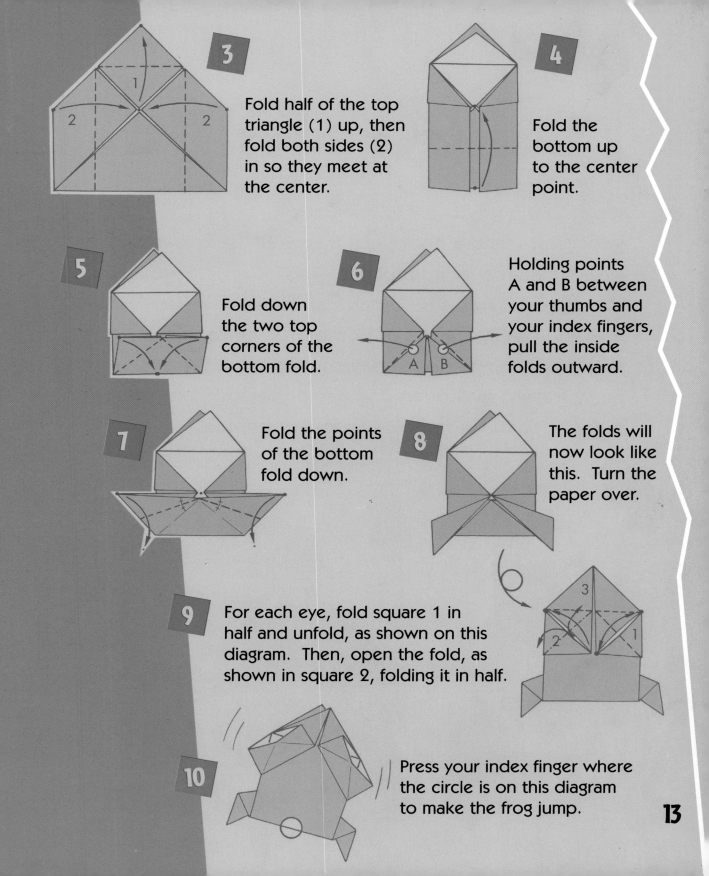

Folded Frame

A photo is a great way to remember good times, and a photo in a frame always makes a wonderful gift. This folded paper frame is so quick and easy to make that you can frame lots of photos. To make them more exciting, use paper of all different colors. Give all your fancy framed photos to one person, as a set, or give just one or two framed photos to lots of people.

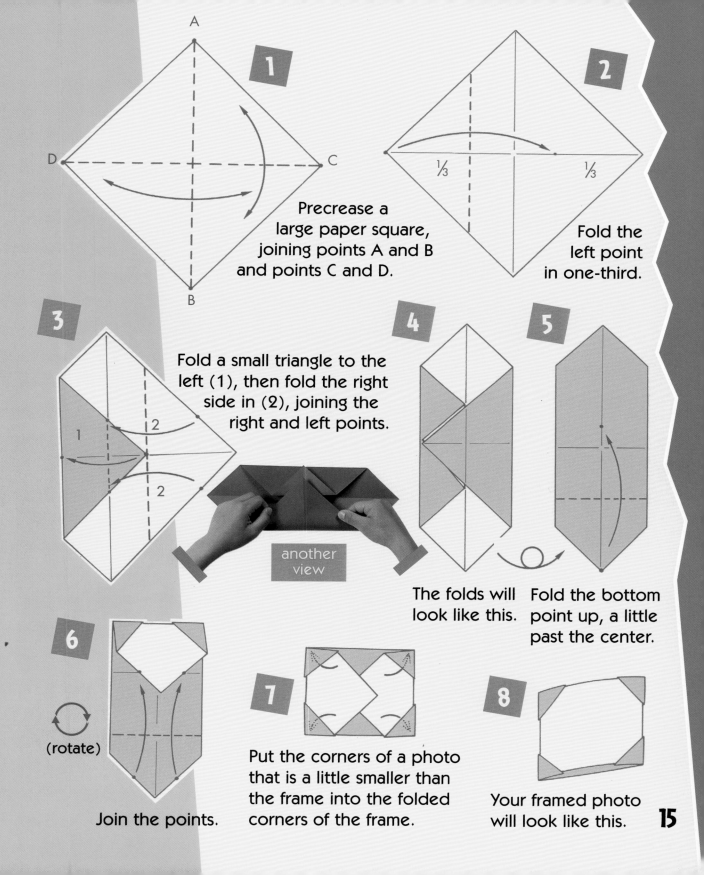

1

Precrease a large paper square, joining points A and B and points C and D.

2

⅓   ⅓

Fold the left point in one-third.

3

Fold a small triangle to the left (1), then fold the right side in (2), joining the right and left points.

1   2

2

another view

4

5

The folds will look like this.

Fold the bottom point up, a little past the center.

6

(rotate)

Join the points.

7

Put the corners of a photo that is a little smaller than the frame into the folded corners of the frame.

8

Your framed photo will look like this.

15

Paper Hens

Even though these paper hens can't cluck, they are still very clever. With only six steps to follow, they look pretty easy to make — but don't let them fool you! These colorful little farmyard figures have some challenging folds.

1 Precrease a valley fold (the center crease). Precrease diagonal mountain folds. To get to step 2, fold in the sides, bringing A and B together.

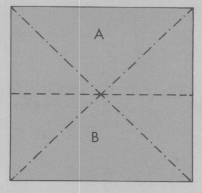

You now have a water bomb base (see page 24) that looks like a pointed hat.

2 (rotate)

Fold the bottom up, joining the points.

3 Unfold the square entirely.

4 Mountain fold the center square and four corner points, as shown.

5 Fold a corner to the middle.

6
1 (head)

A (leg)   2   B (leg)

Unfold corner 1 a little, then fold the middle square in half, following the diagonal valley fold. Bring points A and B together by precreasing each side.

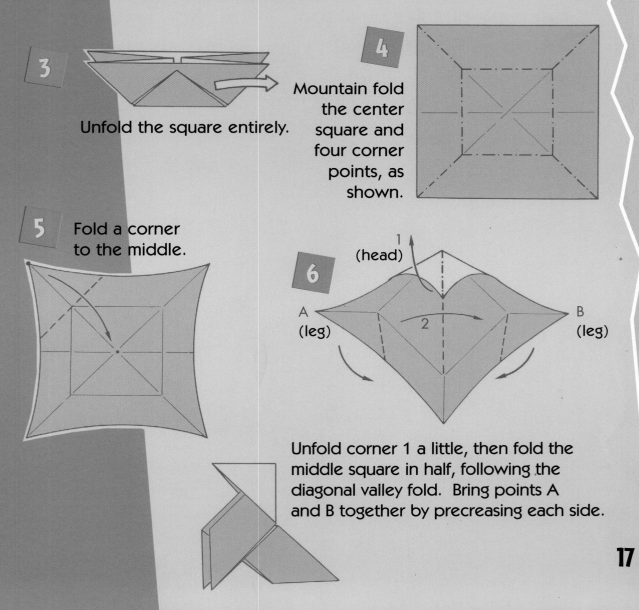

Top Spinner

This spinning toy is a top-notch top — and a lot of fun!
As it spins, the colors of each triangle mix together.
Draw some pictures on it, too.
Then watch what happens
when you spin it. Better
yet, make two top
spinners and have
spinning contests
with a friend.

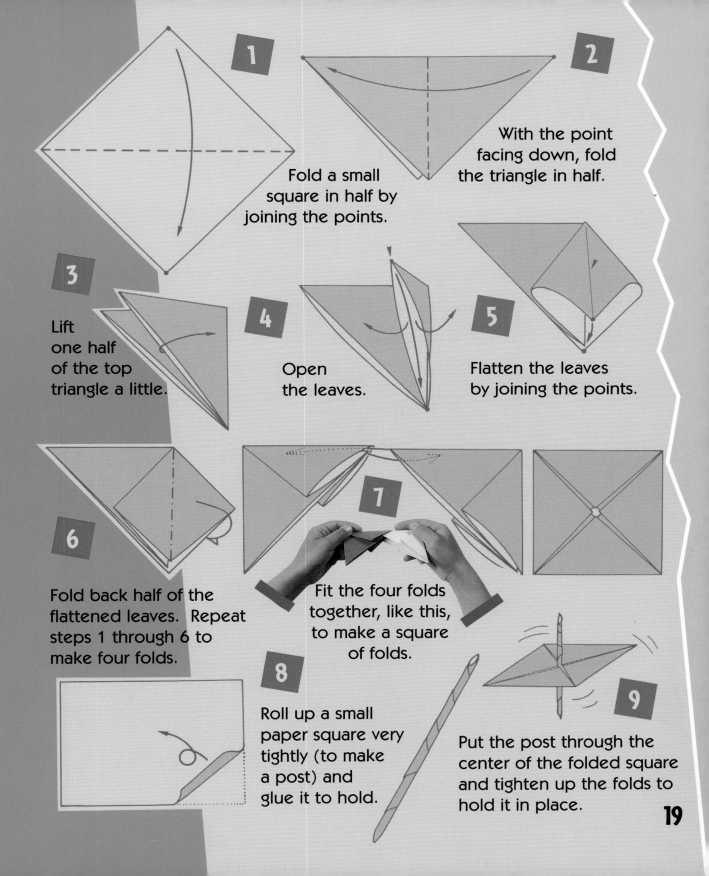

1 Fold a small square in half by joining the points.

2 With the point facing down, fold the triangle in half.

3 Lift one half of the top triangle a little.

4 Open the leaves.

5 Flatten the leaves by joining the points.

6 Fold back half of the flattened leaves. Repeat steps 1 through 6 to make four folds.

7 Fit the four folds together, like this, to make a square of folds.

8 Roll up a small paper square very tightly (to make a post) and glue it to hold.

9 Put the post through the center of the folded square and tighten up the folds to hold it in place.

19

Playful Pups

Big or small, these pups are precious — and their heads can be turned from side to side! You will, however, need two squares of paper to make each pup. Use one square for the body and a separate square for the head. But, don't worry, the folding is easy.

THE BODY

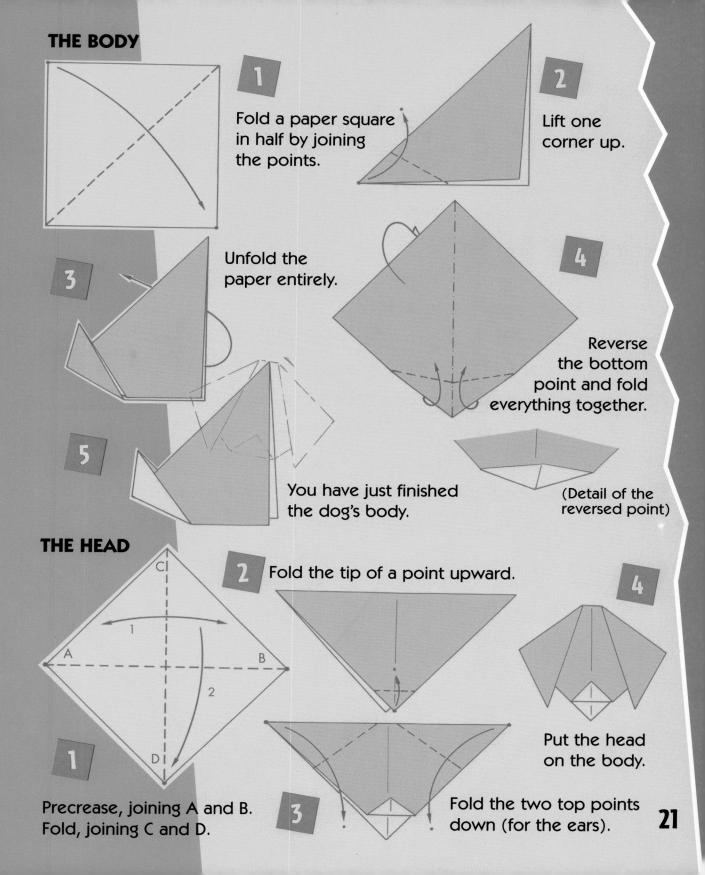

1 Fold a paper square in half by joining the points.

2 Lift one corner up.

3 Unfold the paper entirely.

4 Reverse the bottom point and fold everything together.

(Detail of the reversed point)

5 You have just finished the dog's body.

THE HEAD

1 Precrease, joining A and B. Fold, joining C and D.

2 Fold the tip of a point upward.

3 Fold the two top points down (for the ears).

4 Put the head on the body.

21

Fortune Teller

When can a single square of paper provide hours and hours of fun? When you fold it into a fortune teller! After folding your fortune teller, write eight messages on it (one message under each inside fold) and put a different colored dot on each fold. Then, ask a friend to choose a number. As you count up to the chosen number, open and close the fortune teller with your fingers, first moving it front to back, then side to side. Next, ask your friend to pick a colored dot. Lift up that fold and read the hidden message.

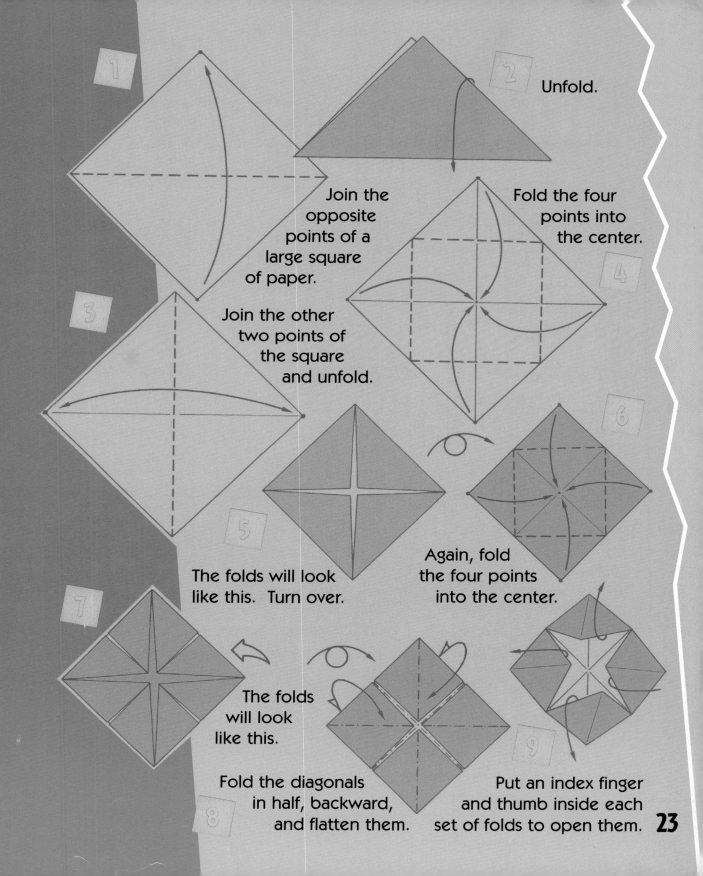

1. Join the opposite points of a large square of paper.

2. Unfold.

3. Join the other two points of the square and unfold.

4. Fold the four points into the center.

5. The folds will look like this. Turn over.

6. Again, fold the four points into the center.

7. The folds will look like this.

8. Fold the diagonals in half, backward, and flatten them.

9. Put an index finger and thumb inside each set of folds to open them.

23

Special Folds

FOLD IN THIRDS

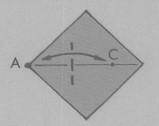

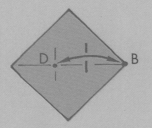

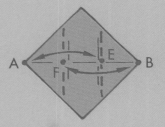

1. Precrease one third, folding A to C.

2. Precrease, folding B to D.

3. Fold A to E and B to F.

WATER BOMB BASE

1. Fold and unfold a paper square in four different directions: horizontally, vertically, diagonally (top left corner to bottom right corner), and diagonally (bottom left corner to top right corner).

2. Using both hands, push the two sides of the horizontal fold toward the center of the square. The top half of the square will collapse over the bottom half.

3. You now have a completed water bomb base.